I0437584

EMPLOYEE FRAUD SCHEMES—AND HOW TO STOP THEM!

EMPLOYEE FRAUD SCHEMES—AND HOW TO STOP THEM!

Lori J. Perry, J.D, M.S., CBM, CFS

Copyright © 2009 by Lori J. Perry, J.D, M.S., CBM, CFS.

ISBN: Softcover   978-1-4415-0743-3

All rights reserved. No part of this book may be reproduced or transmitted in any form or by any means, electronic or mechanical, including photocopying, recording, or by any information storage and retrieval system, without permission in writing from the copyright owner.

This book was printed in the United States of America.

To order additional copies of this book, contact:
Xlibris Corporation
1-888-795-4274
www.Xlibris.com
Orders@Xlibris.com
56537

CONTENTS

PREFACE

Frauds must be stopped. As the statistical information in the Introduction demonstrates, fraud has become pervasive, and its costs are staggering. Our whole society bears the burden of costs from fraud. Some of those costs are monetary—higher insurance rates because of health care frauds, higher taxes because of frauds perpetrated on governments, and higher consumer prices because of frauds against retailers.

But there are also serious social costs associated with frauds. Employees lose their jobs when their companies succumb to massive frauds. Health deteriorates because people can't afford the higher costs of medical care. Confidence in law enforcement declines. Even these subtle costs will eventually be translated into monetary costs to the average citizen and consumer.

The average bank robber might risk his life in an armed confrontation—and risk a long prison sentence—to get away with $20,000. A fraudster can commit his crime in the safety of his office and get away with millions. A former executive with the LTV Corporation, for example, was convicted of taking more than $1.5 million in bribes and kickbacks. He was sentenced to four years and three months in prison.

Although most businesses and organizations investigate suspected frauds, only about two-thirds of frauds are reported to law enforcement agencies. In over a fourth of cases, the organization allows the perpetrators to resign, and in 6% of cases, the organizations admit to simply "hushing up" the fraud! However, according to the U.S. to an executive from the leading audit firm, KPMG, "Although public disclosure may be embarrassing, it could combat or preempt negative publicity, it will demonstrate good faith, close the matter down and protect the organisation's ongoing reputation," Mr Leishman says.

Perpetrators of frauds don't just victimize large corporations with deep pockets, either. A former employee of the Massachusetts Executive Office of Communities and Development was charged with embezzling more than $300,000 earmarked for welfare recipients who performed entry-level tasks to gain job skills.

The examples and recommendations included in this booklet can go a long way toward helping to reduce the risks and costs of frauds in your business. Read them and put them into practice—don't let yourself become a victim of fraud. It's better for you—and better for society—if you aren't.

January 2009

INTRODUCTION

Is your company prepared to face its most formidable challenge? It's *not* your competition. It's *not* inflation. It's *not* product obsolescence. But it's a silent stalker that attacks most organizations today—sometimes ruining them, sometimes crippling them, but always cutting into their profits and productivity.

It's fraud.

The authoritative Association of Certified Fraud Examiners has found that a staggering 95% of United States corporations have been the victims of significant frauds. Most of those frauds were perpetrated by trusted employees or business insiders. The Association has determined that the typical company loses 6% of its annual revenue to fraud and abuse committed by its own management, employees, and suppliers. That's an average of $9 each day per employee.

And fraud is a growth industry. The Association believes that fraud will be the crime of choice for the next century. Why not? It's safe—it isn't violent. Even when perpetrators are caught, they frequently aren't prosecuted so that the company's reputation won't be damaged. And, in terms of sheer pay-off, experts believe that the average fraud outstrips other crimes by 100-to-1.

In a 2006 survey of leading American businesses and organizations, an astounding *21%* of respondents reported *known losses* due to fraud of over $1 million a year! And another 34% reported known losses over $150,000 a year!

Among the types of employee fraud schemes addressed in this book, *average* losses for various types of frauds in 2005 included

- ▶ $450,000 per inventory theft
- ▶ $375,000 per false invoice/vendor scheme
- ▶ $210,000 per diversion of sales scheme
- ▶ $175,000 per expense account abuse
- ▶ $78,000 per unnecessary purchase scheme
- ▶ $53,000 per conflict of interest
- ▶ $47,000 per kickback scheme
- ▶ $38,000 per payroll fraud

Generally, fraud starts small and continues to grow, sometimes threatening an organization's very existence. Once an employee or supplier has breached the controls that are supposed to prevent or detect fraud, and gets away with it, they'll continue to exploit the weakness. Because of fraud's clandestine nature, employers are frequently reluctant to believe it exists. That's especially true in small organizations, where regular interaction among management and employees tends to create an atmosphere of trust. According to Joseph Wells, former FBI agent and now board chairman of the Association of Certified Fraud Examiners,

> "In a study, we found that small businesses are perhaps 100 times more vulnerable to serious fraud than large businesses are. When the boss works face-to-face with

the same people every day, trust becomes built-in. That makes it easier for someone to take advantage."

In the book *The Day America Told the Truth*, researchers reported the results of anonymous surveys of 3,000 Americans on a variety of "taboo" subjects. They claimed that the survey results accurately disclose what people do, think, and feel when no one is watching. They concluded that the top five workplace "crimes" are:

- Pilfering office supplies and equipment,
- Lying to an supervisor or co-worker,
- Stealing company funds,
- Having an affair with a supervisor or co-worker, and
- Taking credit for work not done.

In addition, their surveys found that

- Workers admitted to "goofing off" more than seven hours every week—almost 20% of their paid time.
- Almost half the workers confessed to chronic malingering, calling in sick when they were not—and doing so regularly.
- One in six admitted using drugs or alcohol on the job.

Business consulting firm KPMG's fraud survey reported that 59% of United States businesses and other organizations expected frauds to increase—up from 52% in 2005. Director of KPMG Forensic, Mark Leishman, says, unchecked and undetected, financial fraud is one of the greatest risks to an organisation's viability, as well its reputation and those of its people. Respondents cited economic pressure on employees and inadequate punishment of convicted perpetrators as leading reasons for that expected increase.

Fraud can't be eliminated entirely, but its costs can be reduced. Reducing its cost requires preventative action, starting with a basic understanding of the nature of fraud—how it can happen, what it looks like. Some fraud is well-hidden, but most is not. And *most* frauds can be detected and prevented with common sense and inexpensive solutions. This booklet gives you those solutions.

ORGANIZING TO AVOID FRAUD

Management control for preventing fraud begins with an effective system of checks and balances. KPMG's U.S. Fraud Survey showed that 65 percent of frauds were uncovered through internal audits and the strategy document lists internal audit as one of the most important tools to combat fraud activities. Your accountant, banker, and auditor will call them internal controls, but they're the same things. They are your business' organization and procedures that help you get your job done right, the first time.

If your business has reliable checks and balances—has sound internal controls—you will minimize your errors and opportunities for fraud, and the errors and frauds that might occur will be more likely to be discovered before they become major errors and frauds.

But remember: no organization or system of checks and balances is going to be 100% foolproof. Even if your business had enough people so that one person was doing nothing but checking another person's work, those two could still enter into a collusive arrangement to perpetrate some sort of scheme. If there was a foolproof system of organizing your business to be impervious to fraud, it would be so expensive that it wouldn't be worth having.

The point is to *minimize* your risk of errors and frauds, and to catch the ones that do happen as early as possible. Fortunately, the things that you can do to minimize opportunities for errors and frauds are simple to do and inexpensive to implement.

There are four basic and very straightforward concepts that you need to apply to your organization to get effective management control:

1. *Divide responsibilities among employees so that no one person is responsible for a transaction or event from beginning to end.* This is the single most important element of sound internal control. The person who opens mail shouldn't account for checks, and the person who accounts for checks shouldn't make the bank deposit. The owner of a small business should personally receive the unopened bank statement and scrutinize it for vendors he doesn't recognize, checks made out to people he doesn't know, dual endorsements on the backs of checks, and unusual payment trends. In a small organization, an ideal segregation of duties might not be achievable. When you can't segregate duties properly, try to assign duties so that no one employee is responsible for receiving, handling, recording, and accounting for money from the time it is received until the time it is paid out. Try to bring at least one other employee into the process to break the sequence at one or more points.

2. *Staff your business with qualified, competent, dependable personnel.* Be selective and cautious during your hiring process. Even when a booming economy shrinks the pool of qualified workers, any potential employee who might handle cash should be subjected to a background check adequate to uncover a police record. Blank periods in a job

applicant's work history could mean that time was spent making license plates for the state!

3. *Ensure your operating procedures are well defined, clearly stated (in writing, if they are complicated), understood by personnel, and followed routinely.* Treat employees fairly—employees are often motivated to steal because of dissatisfaction with their jobs. Being denied a raise or promotion, getting an appropriate level of autonomy, or even smaller issues like flexible work hours can lead to thefts as acts of revenge.

4. *Check up on work that is done* by watching operations, verifying calculations and records, and ensuring that personnel are following the prescribed operating procedures.

PREVENTING FRAUD

It is easier to prevent fraud than to detect it. To begin preventing fraud, try to understand the way that a potential perpetrator thinks. Simply increasing the perception that frauds *might* be detected can be effective. Management controls are not optimally effective at deterring fraud if their presence is not known to those who might commit a fraud. Employees should know that management is committed to actively seeking out information concerning internal frauds and thefts.

AWARENESS

Employees should be aware that frauds and thefts *will be punished.* The occasion to commit a fraud is more acceptable psychologically if employees believe that frauds will go undetected and unpunished. New employees should be advised of the policy when they are hired and should acknowledge in writing that they know and understand the policy. Possible punishments, including termination and prosecution, should be clearly communicated. An effective employee awareness policy tells employees what behaviors are acceptable, and what is unacceptable.

REPORTING

Employees should know how and to whom to report suspicious, unethical, or illegal behavior. A system for reporting them should stress that

- Fraud, waste, and abuse occur in nearly all companies.
- Such conduct costs the company jobs and profits.
- The company actively encourages any employee with information to disclose it to the appropriate party.
- The employee can provide the information anonymously and without fear of retaliation for reporting in good faith.
- There is a formal method for reporting—a telephone number, a post office box, or a specified manager.
- The report does not have to be made directly to the employee's supervisors.

RED FLAGS FOR MANAGEMENT

Employees who commit frauds generally use the proceeds to improve their lifestyles. They may buy an expensive car, wear expensive clothing or jewelry, move into a large new home, buy recreational property, or invest heavily. Management should be alert to evidence of employees who appear to live beyond their means. The company should provide training and education to management and employees about fraud. The training should be positive and non accusatory. Illegal conduct eventually penalizes everyone in the company through lost profits, adverse publicity, diminished productivity, and low morale. If management's style is perceived as being conducted fairly and objectively, and if employees know and understand the criteria by which their performance will be evaluated, then the environment will promote honesty—if management is perceived as dishonest, then employees are more likely to be dishonest, too.

Management should offer fair and reasonable compensation. Joseph Wells of the Association of Certified Fraud Examiners stated,

> "As an investigator, I was called in to banks to find out why the tellers were stealing. The banks were putting minimum-wage employees in front of drawers stuffed with money, and then were surprised when someone feels like they have to sneak $50 to keep the lights on."

According to international business consultants KPMG, 66% of respondents to a survey of 5,000 leading United States businesses and organizations identified personal financial pressure as the primary "red flag" warning of potential frauds. Other red flags cited were

- vices (substance abuse and gambling),
- extravagant purchases and lifestyles,
- real or imagined grievances against the employer,
- continuing transactions with related parties,
- increased stress,

- internal pressure from management, and
- short vacations or unusual working hours.

REWARDS

Some companies have policies for giving rewards for information leading to the recovery of merchandise, property, or money. Others offer rewards upon the criminal conviction of persons involved in the scheme. If you consider this policy, be sure to have it carefully reviewed by your legal counsel. The amount of the reward can vary from a fixed amount to a percentage of the recovery. *Crime Stoppers* recommends that awards not exceed $1,000.

MINIMIZE PRESSURE ON EMPLOYEES

Pressures from the work environment drive many perpetrators to commit their frauds. Reduce job-related pressures on employees by having an open-door policy—if employees feel like they can express their concerns and problems, pressures can be alleviated before they become critical. Have an employee support program to provide assistance for substance abuse, gambling addictions, marital and financial problems, and similar external pressures.

REMEMBER . . .

Symptoms or appearances of fraud may be present, even though a fraud isn't! Don't jump to conclusions—the cost of mishandling a fraud could exceed the loss itself. If you believe a fraud has occurred, consult a professional right away. Consult with your auditor or a government criminal investigative unit that specializes in fraud investigations, or contact the Association of Certified Fraud Examiners at 800-245-3321 for a referral to a qualified professional.

CASH FRAUD SCHEMES

Cash is the most liquid of assets and offers the greatest temptation for theft and embezzlement. However, frauds involving cash are usually *smaller* than fraud schemes involving other assets—because companies tend to have more stringent and effective controls over cash and tend to make sure that employees comply strictly with those controls. Cash frauds can be either on-books (involving erroneous recording of transactions in the accounting records) or off-books (involving failures to record transactions in the accounting records). Long experience has demonstrated that fraud schemes involving cash generally follow these basic patterns.

SKIMMING

Skimming is the theft of cash from the business before it can be recorded in the accounting system. That is, the receipt of cash is never reported. Examples of skimming are ringing up transactions on cash registers for less than the amount received from the customer, or simply failing to ring up the transaction at all. Skimming is a particular concern at retail operations (like fast-food restaurants) where most transactions are conducted in small amounts of cash and customers have little incentive to obtain or examine receipts.

Prevention: Separate employees' duties so that the person who receives cash gives the customer a receipt or ticket that must be presented to another employee to actually obtain the merchandise purchased. Also, consider giving customers their purchases for free if they fail to receive a receipt or are charged the wrong price. This will encourage customers to examine their receipts—and makes them part of your internal controls.

VOIDS

Fraud by voids occurs when an employee records a sales transaction, then voids the sale and removes cash from the register, as if no transaction had occurred. Retailing operations, selling merchandise with very low unit prices in small lots where inventory is not closely monitored (for example, a hardware store selling bulk nuts and bolts from bins) are especially susceptible to fraud by voids.

Prevention: Separate employees' duties so that a supervisor is required to approve cashiers' voided transactions.

UNDER-RINGS

There are two ways to perpetrate frauds through under-rings, or recording transactions at less than their actual amount. The first is to record sales at unauthorized discounts—for example, a cashier receives the full retail price of merchandise from a customer, but records the sale as if the customer were entitled to a discount, such as are frequently offered to employees, children, or senior citizens. The cashier simply pockets the difference between the actual retail sale and the discounted sale price. Another way to perpetrate fraud through under-rings occurs when a cashier or salesperson sells merchandise to a collaborator at a discount. The collaborator then returns the merchandise for a refund at the full retail price.

Prevention: Require that sales at discounts must be approved by a supervisor and that original cash receipts must accompany refunds on returned merchandise. Also, consider giving customers their purchases for free if they fail to receive an accurate receipt. That will make both the cashier and the customer integral parts of your internal control system.

SUBSTITUTING CHECKS FOR CASH

This is a form of unauthorized "borrowing" from the company. An employee misappropriates cash in his custody by taking the cash from his register or cash drawer and substituting his own check. The substitution check is replaced periodically so that, on any given day, there is a current check substituted for the cash previously removed, and the balance of the cash for which the employee is responsible agrees with the his authorized accountability. This type of fraud occurs often when employees are allowed to keep their own cash drawers and remit only the day's receipts.

Prevention: require that each employee handling cash have his own assigned cash drawer, and that those cash drawers be independently reconciled by a different employee at the end of each day and then turned over to a custodian for depositing the day's receipts intact.

ALTERING CASH RECEIPTS

This type of fraud occurs most often in small businesses, where there are fewer employees among whom to segregate cash-handling duties. If the same person is responsible for both receiving and depositing the day's receipts, then he can divert funds from the deposits and alter the deposit documents to conceal the theft. The person who reconciles the bank statement will not detect the diversion, because the deposit documents will equal the bank's recorded deposits. In a typical business, even payments that have been posted to customers' accounts can be subjected to this kind of diversion—the person who makes the deposit can alter the total amount of the cash receipts and the amount actually deposited. When the difference between the totals posted to customer accounts and the actual deposits is noticed (usually during a reconciliation process, long after the alterations have occurred), that difference is usually written off as an unreconciled (read: "unexplained") accounting adjustment.

Prevention: Separate employee duties so that persons who either take in cash receipts or reconcile the bank statement never prepare and make the deposit. Examine register tapes closely for evidence of alterations—including those that render them illegible—and note trends of errors, refunds, and discounts among different persons handling cash.

FICTITIOUS REFUNDS AND DISCOUNTS

These occur when an employee—who does not necessarily handle any cash, but might only have access to the accounting records—records a transaction as if a refund was given, but no merchandise was returned, or when a discount is made although none was approved. The employee then misappropriates funds equal to the amount of the fictitious refund or discount. For example, an employee may issue refund checks to actual customers, but intercept the checks and endorse them over to himself or to a fictitious identity for which he has established a bank account, and deposit the checks to his own account.

Prevention: To prevent discounts to fictitious persons, require either that discounts be independently approved in writing before they are offered; or require that sufficient documented information be obtained from the person receiving the discount (such as driver license number, home address, and phone number) to allow a subsequent independent verification of his eligibility for the discount, and follow up on those on a test basis. To prevent fictitious refunds, require that requests for refunds be accompanied by the original sales advice and that refund checks be countersigned by another employee not otherwise involved in the refund process.

KITING

Kiting is the process of recording cash in multiple bank accounts when the cash is actually either in transit or does not exist at all. Kiting schemes are possible only when a bank allows its customers to withdraw funds that the bank has not yet collected from another bank. Kiting schemes require that banks pay on unfunded deposits—that is, customers' deposits that have not cleared the customers' banks and been credited to the new depository. Kiting can be perpetrated using multiple accounts at one bank, or using multiple accounts at multiple banks. With the expanded use of bank wires for transferring funds, kiting schemes can be accomplished with great frequency and rapidity.

Prevention: Bank statements should be promptly and regularly reconciled by an employee not involved in the deposit or payment processes. The reconciliation should include identifying deposits and transfers in transit on the account's cut-off date. Deposits in one account should be associated with withdrawals in another account on the same day—there should be no lapses between dates of deposit and dates of withdrawals.

MISSING DOCUMENTS

Certain missing documents—especially checks and items used in bank reconciliations—should be red flags warning of potential frauds. Voided checks might indicate that employees have embezzled cash—when the embezzlement is charged to expense accounts, the checks can be voided and removed from distribution points.

Prevention: Critical documents should be serially pre-numbered, and manually prepared originals should generate self-carbon copies. The entire sequence of documents should be accounted for; all original pages of voided documents should be left in the sequential file.

ACCOUNTS RECEIVABLE SCHEMES

LAPPING

Lapping is the concealment of an employee's original misappropriation of cash. In this scheme, the employee diverts cash received from a customer, at a later time, another customer's payment is credited to the first customer's account. The shortage in the second customer's account is covered by receipts from a third customer, and so on. That is, the shortage in Customer A's account is made up by Customer B's payment; the shortage in Customer B's account is made up by Customer C's payment. The funds so diverted may be directed toward other business expenses, and may not be actually stolen by the employee. The delay in the application of customer payments continues until the scheme is detected, until the cash is restored, or the scheme is covered up by credits to the proper customer and a fictitious charge is made to other accounts.

Prevention: Lapping can be detected by periodically comparing the dates of customers' payments with the dates those payments are posted to the customers' subledgers. Segregate duties in the receipt of payments by having one employee prepare a control listing of receipts to be posted to customer accounts by another employee. Each day, verify that total postings to customer accounts agree with the control total of receipts. If you receive a large volume of customer receipts through the mail, consider entering into a lock-box arrangement with your bank, so that customers can send their payments directly to your bank.

WRITING OFF ACCOUNTS RECEIVABLE

In this scheme, an employee diverts payments received on delinquent accounts, inactive accounts, or accounts that had previously been written off as uncollectible. Many companies typically do not keep close track of such accounts, and such diversions may readily go undetected.

Prevention: Segregate employees' duties so that no one employee writes off accounts as uncollectible, receives payments, and posts them to the customers' accounts. Again, if you receive a large volume of customer receipts by mail, consider entering into a lock-box arrangement with your bank.

FICTITIOUS ACCOUNTS RECEIVABLE

When an employee's compensation is based on sales, rather than on collections or a combination of both, there is an incentive for him to fabricate sales, with their corresponding accounts receivable, to inflate his apparent sales and the resulting commissions. To conceal this scheme, sales transactions may be reversed in the accounting records in a subsequent period.

Prevention: Associate employees' commissions with actual collections, not with sales alone. Include such factors as customer returns and allowances within reasonable norms. Examining sales returns and reversals at the beginning of an accounting period will help to detect this scheme.

INVENTORY SCHEMES

THEFT OF CONVERTIBLE DOCUMENTS

Documents, as well as merchandise, are susceptible to theft from inventory. Your inventory of negotiable documents—tickets, vouchers, blank check stock—is a tempting asset for frauds because they can be easily converted to cash. If multiple employees have access to the inventory, and if accountability is not strictly fixed and monitored, a theft can go undetected.

Prevention: Provide tight physical security over these documents—keep them in a safe, in a locking cash drawer, or in a locked closet, and keep the room where they are stored locked when it is not occupied. Assign responsibility for the inventory of these documents, and allow physical access to them, to the fewest number of persons feasible. Maintain accurate records of the inventory—additions, issues, and losses—and conduct frequent surprise inventories of them to verify their presence and sequence.

THEFT OF DELIVERED MATERIALS

A common form of theft requires collusion between an employee and a delivery agent. The employee responsible for receiving goods can sign the agent's delivery ticket to falsely acknowledge receipt of more goods than were actually received. The outside agent will then sell the stolen goods and share the proceeds with his employee accomplice.

Prevention: Most collusive arrangements are difficult to detect and prevent. This one can be deterred by having a second employee—usually an inventory custodian—in turn take the goods delivered from the receiving employee and verify the count and receive reporting before taking the goods into inventory. Examine receiving reports closely for evidence of alterations. If goods are not taken into a formal inventory system, but are expensed at acquisition, responsibility for receiving the deliveries should be rotated among employees to prevent the development of close relationships with delivery agents.

THEFT OF SCRAP MATERIALS

Materials can be stolen by being improperly written off as scrap or surplus. Good or serviceable equipment and materials may then be diverted to a scrap storage area and subsequently retrieved and sold. Control over materials designated as scrap or surplus are generally not as effective as controls over materials in use.

Prevention: Appoint a specific employee as custodian of materials designated for disposal. Treat dispositions of scrap or surplus just as if it were an inventory of goods. Require that all equipment or goods having a value in excess of a designated amount must be written off by two employees and prominently tagged for storage until disposal. Areas where materials designated for disposal are stored should be kept physically secure. File insurance claims on any missing assets—the insurance company's investigation may disclose other weaknesses in your control systems.

EMBEZZLEMENTS CHARGED TO INVENTORY

Embezzlement can be concealed through an inventory expense account; that is, the theft is charged to inventory expense. Inventories generally experience some variances because of waste, loss, pilferage, and ordinary errors, so an embezzlement can go undetected until the inventory account is reconciled. Even then, the evidence of the embezzlement may be obscured by time and documentation errors.

Prevention: Use an automated system to account for inventory. Automated records facilitate certain types of analyses that can help to detect this kind of fraud—and the evidence of such controls may deter this type of fraud. Investigate any unexplained entries in the inventory records—ensure that they are substantiated by source documents, such as receiving reports or sales invoices.

THEFT OF INVENTORY

The simplest fraud is theft of inventory. Perpetrators may try to conceal such thefts through falsified records (such as changing counts on inventory issue forms or receiving reports), or they may simply expect that the thefts will go undetected until a physical inventory is taken, and then be written off as shrinkage or spoilage.

Prevention: Ensure that the system of forms used to account for inventory receipts and issues is properly designed, with sufficient information, copies, and files to fix responsibility. Conduct surprise inventory counts at irregular intervals and reconcile any differences. To be conducted efficiently, such surprise inventories can be directed toward only those inventory items that are susceptible to theft—high unit cost items or readily convertible items. Inspect inventory forms closely for evidence of alterations. Require that all writing on inventory documents be in ink.

PURCHASING SCHEMES

FICTITIOUS INVOICES

A fictitious invoice is one that does not represent a legitimate sale and purchase. Fictitious invoices can take many forms—the vendors may not actually exist, or fictitious invoices may be altered or falsified invoices from a legitimate vendor. Fictitious invoices can be used to submit phony or inflated billings.

OVER-BILLING

Frauds involving altered or inflated invoices generally require that an employee of the organization being invoiced work in collusion with the vendor. For example, the vendor may bill for more goods or services than were delivered, or may bill at a higher price than agreed; or the employee may alter the vendor's original invoice to reflect higher prices or more goods or services delivered. The employee then facilitates payment to the vendor by approving either the invoice (when it used as a receiving report) or the authorization for payment, and the employee splits the profits with his accomplice.

Prevention: Require that receiving reports be prepared for all goods and services, and that employees authorized to approve payments to vendors are not otherwise involved in the procurement or receiving processes. Require that payments be authorized only when the receiving report has been matched to the vendor's invoice. Pay only from vendors' original invoices and inspect them for evidence of alteration, such as overstrikes, smudged or illegible amounts, or extension and footing errors.

FICTITIOUS VENDORS

An employee in a position to authorize payments to vendors may establish a falsified identity or front operation posing as a vendor, either alone or in collusion with someone else. The employee, as a falsified vendor, then invoices the company for goods or services and approves payment. Employees perpetrating this fraud may be sophisticated enough to establish mailing addresses different from their own, to use bank accounts established in the name of the fictitious vendor, and to use customized invoice forms.

Prevention: Separating duties in the receiving and payment processes will deter this fraud. In addition, establish and maintain a list of authorized vendors for commonly-purchased commodities and require that vendors be added to the list only with the independent approval of a designated purchasing agent. Require that vendors provide street addresses—don't accept post office box numbers only. Periodically compare lists of vendors' addresses to employees' addresses and investigate any duplicates.

EXCESSIVE PURCHASES OF PROPERTY

This form of fictitious invoicing ordinarily requires that the perpetrator liquidate the supplies or inventory purchased. To accomplish that, the supplies or inventory must be moved from the organization's premises or delivered initially to a different location. Deliveries may be made to the employee's own residence or to another location under his control (such as another business).

Prevention: Ensure that record-keeping for inventory and assets is adequate to provide accountability and that custodial controls over inventory and assets are adequate to prevent unauthorized removal from the premises. Maintain a list of authorized receiving locations and investigate any invoices or receiving reports that do not match locations on the list.

EXCESSIVE PROCUREMENT OF SERVICES

Services are deliverable in many forms—such as legal advice, financial planning, strategic planning, and architectural designs. Documentation for receiving services is usually different from documents evidencing delivery of supplies, equipment, or inventory. For example, procurements of services generally do not generate receiving reports. Billings for services are generally not specific as to amounts, the nature of services provided on a given date or at a given time, or even who in particular provided the services. It may then be difficult to determine whether the services being billed were for the benefit of the organization or for an individual.

Prevention: The ability of middle-managers and supervisors to enter into contracts without management's approval should be severely limited. Require that all contracts for services be approved by upper management and that the scope of services be described in the contract as specifically as possible. If possible, payments should be associated with "deliverables," as when a contract requires the production of documents (such as architectural plans). The deliverables should be associated with specific dates for completion. The contract should include an upset limit, one that cannot be exceeded without the execution of a new or amended contract. Scan histories of payments to service providers for patterns of contract amounts that are just under limits requiring additional authorizations, and review contract files for evidence of unauthorized changes to either the scope of the work or upset limits.

CHECKS PAYABLE TO EMPLOYEES

Employees involved in the payment process may be in a position to divert payments intended for vendors to themselves or to external entities under their control, including relatives. Employees may be able to change payee names on checks. In such cases, an employee may be able to deposit a check to his own account without question. In other cases, an employee only needs to get physical custody of a check still payable to a vendor. He can change mailing addresses, or simply divert checks before they are mailed. As unsophisticated as it may seem, there have been times when employees have deposited checks plainly payable to another entity into their personal bank accounts.

Prevention: Use check stock that is self-duplicating. Limit employees' access to vendor information. Require that checks exceeding a prescribed amount must be countersigned in ink by an officer. Establish a procedure that ensures that checks are put into sealed envelopes immediately after preparation and mailed promptly by someone who is not otherwise involved in the receiving or payment processes. Periodically compare employees' mailing addresses to vendors' and investigate any duplications.

DUPLICATED PAYMENTS

Most payment systems are sufficiently sophisticated to prevent duplicated payments to vendors, but an employee may be in a position to override procedures designed to prevent them. Frauds involving duplicated payments generally require that an employee work in collusion with an accomplice in the vendor's organization. However, the employee may be able to intercept the outgoing payment and divert the check to his own account. When an employee works with an accomplice, the accomplice is generally aware of the duplicated payment and shares the proceeds with the employee who facilitated the duplication.

Prevention: Require that vendor's original invoices accompany all requests for disbursements—do not authorize disbursements based on duplicated invoices. Invalidate paid invoices by stamping them "paid," perforating them, or otherwise distinctively marking them so that they cannot be re-used. Use an automated accounts payable system having fields for input of vendors' invoice data—the invoice number, date, amount, and requisition or stock number. Automated systems can easily identify potentially duplicated payments by flagging disbursements having the same invoice number and amount. Segregate duties among employees so that the person who is responsible for mailing payment checks to vendors has no other duties in the receipt, payment, or accounting procedures.

CONFLICTS OF INTEREST

A conflict of interest occurs when an employee at any level in the organization has an undisclosed economic interest in a transaction, and that undisclosed interest adversely affects the organization that he works for. For example, an employee or a member of his immediate household may own a business that supplies goods or services to his employer. If the employee is a purchasing agent, he may steer his employer's business toward his conflicting ownership without disclosing the relationship to his employer—and the transactions involved in that business may negatively impact the employer. Note that conflicts of interest do not necessarily require that the employer incur actual damage or loss—only that the *potential* for such damage or loss be present in the undisclosed relationship. Losses arising from conflicts of interest generally occur from goods or services paid for but not delivered or from goods or services paid for at inflated prices. These schemes also frequently involve the receipt of "gifts" from vendors and contractors.

Conflicts of interest involve collusive arrangements, which are very difficult to protect your organization against because they violate the principle of segregation of duties. That principle assumes that two persons act independently of each other to execute their fiduciary, agent, or employee responsibilities in the interests of their principles or employers. In conflicts of interest, the employee or agent asserts his interests, or persons acting in collusion assert their interests, over their employers or principles.

SERVICES OR GOODS NOT PROVIDED

Frauds caused by undisclosed conflicts of interest is when an employee authorizes or facilitates payment for services not actually rendered or for goods not actually provided. This may occur when the provider of goods or services is a relative or associate of the employee. The employee may falsely acknowledge receipt of goods or services not actually provided; may authorize payment for such undelivered goods or services. These types of frauds generally require collusive arrangements between the employee and a relative, associate, or a controlled business entity. Billings paid by the employer are then divided among the collusive parties to the arrangement.

Prevention: Frauds arising from conflicts of interest can be deterred by rotating duties among employees to the extent possible, so that employees' business relationships with external parties do not become close over a long term. For example, if multiple employees are responsible for purchasing supplies and equipment, change their buying assignments by vendor or commodity. Ensure that your employment screening process is thorough—especially if you are filling a position of significant trust and responsibility. Require applicants to disclose their business interests and those of members of their immediate household. Do a thorough background check on prospective new employees before you hire them—get their authorization for you to review their credit history, criminal background, and employment history. Be alert to discrepancies between their disclosures and the results of the check. Observe current employees—do they appear to be living a lifestyle that their wages obviously would not support? If so, investigate as appropriate.

INVESTMENT SCHEMES

USING COMPANY ASSETS AS COLLATERAL

Employees with access to company assets and proofs of ownership can present the asset as collateral for their borrowing. For example, an employee having access to the company's certificates of deposit or vehicle registrations can present them to a lender for collateral. This scheme will work whether or not the lender maintains custody of the asset or proof of ownership, but it is difficult to detect if the lender does not maintain custody. The employee's borrowing results in the pledge of a company asset for collateral for his loan. The employee may then default on the loan, and the business may either lose the asset or become engaged in litigation over it.

Prevention: Obtain and hold in a secured place all negotiable instruments (certificates of deposit, stocks, bonds, and notes receivable) and all proofs of ownership of significant assets (titles and registrations). Restrict physical access to them and keep them in a fireproof safe or vault. Assign responsibility for them to a specific employee; and periodically have their continued presence independently verified. Institute and enforce a system for the assets' custodian to log them in and out of custody, so that the person currently having possession of them is always determinable.

ACCOUNT TRANSFERS

Cash on deposit may not be earning interest for your company. It may be subject to unauthorized use by employees. For example, your company may be required to maintain a compensating cash balance in an account. If an employee can transfer these funds to and from different institutions, he may be able to "borrow" the funds and earn interest on them. The purpose of this form of fraud is not to misappropriate the funds themselves, but to earn interest on them. Companies required to keep accounts in other states or countries are especially susceptible to this form of abuse.

Prevention: Ensure that your agreements with a depository require the written authorization of two company officers to make transfers or other changes to accounts, and require that the depository confirm the authorization with a third official. Examine statements of income and expense from the depository for unexplained fluctuations.

FIXED ASSET SCHEMES

THEFT

Fixed assets are generally not easily movable or convertible, but many are subject to theft by employees. For example, an employee may report his assigned vehicle as stolen, either while it was left unattended or pursuant to a falsified criminal incident.

Prevention: Report all thefts to the police and file claims against them with your insurer. Their investigations may disclose criminal activity. Be sure that your employees know the policy and that it will always be followed. Prosecute all known instances of theft—a failure to prosecute or otherwise deal with an employee's criminal activity could jeopardize your fidelity bonding.

ORDINARY PERSONAL USE

Employees' use of business assets for personal purposes is one of the most common forms of fraud. These schemes range from using photocopiers to duplicate personal documents to using company phones to make international long-distance calls.

Prevention: Abuses of company assets for personal use are generally failures of supervision—employees can be expected to take advantage of lax supervision. Establish reasonable and realistic policies for dealing with incidents of personal use of business assets like telephones and copiers. For example, provide that photocopiers may be used for a reasonable volume of personal use if the employees provide their own copy paper, but be alert for signs of abuse of the policy—such as excessive repair and maintenance costs. Allow reasonable use of phones for personal calls, provided that employees reimburse costs of long-distance calls or other special charges. Assign responsibility for assets—including photocopiers—to a specific employee and hold him accountable for their use. After the policies have been established and publicized, hold managers and supervisors responsible for enforcing them.

DISPOSAL OF FIXED ASSETS

Even fully-depreciated assets, such as a production machine that has been replaced, are assets that represent potential cash flow from their disposal by sale. Assets that have been removed from production and set aside awaiting disposition may be stolen by employees if control over surplus equipment is inadequate. An employee can realize some gain from an illegal conversion of a fixed asset, whether for salvage or scrap value.

Prevention: Treat assets designated for disposal like an inventory of goods, and appoint an employee as a custodian over the inventory of assets to be disposed. Require documentation for the change in custody and for an accounting of the proceeds from each asset designated for disposal. Physically separate assets designated for disposal from other assets—in a secured area, just as you would secure an inventory of goods. Take periodic inventories of fixed assets that are still in use, and conduct unannounced physical inventories of equipment (on a sample basis, if there are a large number of assets) giving special attention to those assets that are easily moveable or readily convertible.

DISPOSAL OF NEGOTIABLE ASSETS

When a negotiable asset, such as stock, is designated for sale, an employee may be in a position to profit from either diverting the asset, the proceeds from its disposition, or fees associated with its disposition. Such schemes may involve alterations of documents used in the process, such as changing the number of shares of stock liquidated, or changing the dollar amount on a certificate of deposit. An employee may enter into a collusive arrangement with an external party to pay inflated service charges or fees, and share the proceeds.

Prevention: Carefully examine all documents used in transactions involving negotiable instruments. Look for evidence of alterations, like smudges or inconsistencies in the documents. Reconcile the proceeds, including fees and charges withheld by agents, to the asset's selling price. If possible, arrange to have negotiable assets held in trust, so that the trustee can keep custody of the negotiable assets and handle purchases and sales. Have the trustee deposit proceeds from sales directly into your account and provide you with a statement. The trustee should provide you with a periodic statement of assets held—compare the statements from period to period, and reconcile transactions to your account.

PAYROLL FRAUDS

GHOST EMPLOYEES

A "ghost" employee is a fictitious one, one that doesn't exist. No services are received in exchange for the payment to the "ghost." Employees who are in positions to add persons to the payroll, such as managers who hire laborers, may be in a position to generate the documents required to add employees to the company's payroll. If the manager is also responsible for distributing employees' paychecks, he can then divert the ghost employee's paycheck by simply endorsing it to himself, or he may have it directly deposited to an account that he controls in the name of the ghost employee. If checks are mailed to employees, the manager may submit his own or an accomplice's address on the documents used to authorize the addition to the payroll.

Prevention: Segregate the payroll distribution function from payroll preparation—employee paychecks should be distributed by someone who is not otherwise involved in the personnel or payroll processes. Consider issuing company access passes or identification cards with employee photos and require that they be presented to obtain a paycheck. Examine the endorsements on employees' paid paychecks for endorsement to another employee.

ABUSE OF OVERTIME PAY

Employees that are responsible for reporting their own overtime may inflate the hours they actually worked and receive wages in excess of those actually earned. Overtime frauds are frequently collusive arrangements between employees and supervisors who are responsible for approving overtime—the employees may kick back a portion of their unearned overtime compensation to the supervisor who approved it for payment.

Prevention: Require that overtime be approved in advance by a responsible manager and be incurred for specific activities. Verify that productivity is consistent with overtime claimed. Be alert to unusual patterns of overtime, such as one employee or one work group claiming a disproportionate amount of overtime.

MISAPPROPRIATING WITHHOLDING TAXES

An employee responsible for paying state, federal, or trust account taxes may temporarily "borrow" payments until the date they are required to be deposited. Your company may then lose a couple of days' "float"—interest earned on the cash in your account—or you might incur penalties if the employee makes the payment late. The employee might deposit the payment to his own account, where it will accrue interest earnings, until the date the deposit of taxes is required.

Prevention: Arrange with your bank to have payroll taxes transferred by wire to the appropriate agency on the business day that they are due, and provide you with a confirmation of the transfer.

REIMBURSEMENT FOR PERSONAL EXPENSES

Employees who are reimbursed for expenses incurred for the company, such as travel and training, may submit fraudulent expenses for reimbursement. Those may be personal expenses, not related to company business, or they may be expenses in excess of a reasonable cost. Employees who have company credit cards might charge personal expenses to them, or might make purchases seemingly for company business, and then return the merchandise for a cash refund. Travel arrangements might be made to accommodate personal affairs by circuitous routing or by days of travel in excess of the number actually required. Perquisites, such as frequent-flyer awards earned while traveling on company business, may be kept for personal use. Personal long-distance calls might be claimed as employee business expenses.

Prevention: Review employees' expense reports before reimbursing them. Require that employees claiming reimbursement for business expenses present original invoices or bills itemizing the nature of the expenses. Inspect or take custody of all materials, supplies, and equipment charged to the company. To promote economic travel arrangements, consider paying employees per diem rates for lodging and meals while traveling on company business, rather than reimbursing specific costs. Require employees to get multiple quotes for airline, ship, or rail travel and for rental vehicles. If your business requires considerable travel, inquire of travel agents, airlines, and other providers about standard pricing agreements or discounts from list prices. If employees claim reimbursement for entertainment expenses, require that they provide the date, time, amount, and business purpose of the expense.

INTERNAL CONTROL CHECKLIST

☑
To get an idea of just how good your internal controls are, fill out this questionnaire. If your controls and procedures are in place and working, then you should be able to answer *"yes"* to most questions. If you have to answer "no" to several questions, then you may need to make some changes to reduce your exposure to risks of fraud. This checklist is not intended to be complete, but it does include the most critical elements of internal control.

Internal Control	Yes	No
Are policies and procedures documented and organized in an up-to-date, current manual that is readily accessible to all employees?		
Are employees' duties and responsibilities documented in written job descriptions?		
Are employees covered by appropriate amounts of theft, dishonesty, and disappearance bonds?		

Internal Control	Yes	No
Do employees have skills and training necessary for performing their jobs satisfactorily?		
Is the work load current, with no significant backlog of work?		
Is there an inventory of tangible assets that is verified periodically by the designated employee?		
Are descriptive receipts issued to customers for all cash and checks received?		
Are receipts sequentially pre-numbered and generated in at least three parts?		
Are copies of the receipts distributed to the accounting office and to the sales office?		
Are receipts issued compared to other supporting documents to verify the accuracy of the amounts?		
Are unissued receipts adequately secured to prevent loss or theft?		
Are checks received immediately stamped with restrictive endorsements for deposit only?		

Internal Control	Yes	No
Are cash and checks received adequately safeguarded until being deposited in the bank?		
Does each employee receiving cash have a separate cash register or drawer?		
Is access to the cash registers or drawers restricted to those persons assigned responsibility for them?		
Is each employee's cash register or drawer balanced out daily and independently verified by an employee who does not receive cash?		
Does an employee who does not receive money prepare the bank deposit?		
Are cash receipts deposited intact daily?		
Are receipts periodically compared to other copies of the same receipts and to the bookkeeping entries to ensure that the amounts recorded are the same?		
Is incoming mail opened daily by an employee who does not take in over-the-counter receipts?		
Does the person opening the mail prepare a list of cash and checks received?		

Internal Control	Yes	No
Is there a system to account for installment or periodic payments?		
Are all customers' outstanding account balances known and recorded with a controlling total?		
Is there a system to keep up with when customers' payments are due?		
Is the controlling total of customers' outstanding balances periodically compared to the subsidiary customer accounts?		
Are all disbursements made only by sequentially pre-numbered checks?		
Are all unused checks accounted for and physically safeguarded?		
Are disbursement checks prepared only after substantiating documentation has been presented and verified?		
Are checks prepared only be an employee who is not responsible for the bookkeeping function?		
Is the payee line completed on all checks before they are approved and signed?		

Internal Control	Yes	No
Are checks prohibited from being made payable to "cash" or "bearer"?		
Are outgoing checks mailed promptly without being returned to an employee who approves them for payment or accounts for them?		
Are documents used to substantiate payments voided to prevent their re-use?		
Are bank account balances protected by provisions of the depository agreement and/or by limits of FDIC coverage?		
Are bank statements promptly reconciled by an employee other than one who prepares bank deposits and approves disbursement checks?		
Are deposits shown on the bank statements agreed to the accounting records as to date and amount?		
Are bank service charges verified as to amount?		
Are canceled checks examined for alterations, unauthorized signatures, and irregular endorsements?		

Internal Control	Yes	No
Are completed bank reconciliations reviewed and approved by an employee other than the one who performed the original reconciliation?		
Are entries in the accounting records made promptly from appropriate source documents, such as receipts, check copies, and invoices?		
Are entries in the accounting records made by an employee who is not responsible for receiving cash, preparing bank deposits, and approving disbursements?		
Are entries in the accounting records periodically reviewed by someone other than the person who initially recorded them, and are those entries compared with the source documents that substantiate them?		
Are inventory records independently verified periodically by physical counts of items in inventory?		

www.ingramcontent.com/pod-product-compliance
Lightning Source LLC
Chambersburg PA
CBHW031331290526
45784CB00014B/2547